© **2020** Adalina Giammatteo. All rights reserved. No part of this book may be reproduced or transmitted in any form or by any means, electronic or mechanical, including photocopying, recording, or by any information storage and retrieval system, without written permission from the author, except for the inclusion of brief quotations in a review.

Inferno Publishing Company

Houston, TX

Book design by Giacomo Giammatteo

This edition was prepared by Giacomo Giammatteo gg@giacomog.com

❀ Created with Vellum

THE YEAR OF 2020

ADALINA GIAMMATTEO

FORWARD BY GIACOMO GIAMMATTEO

My eight-year-old granddaughter wrote this herself. It was her idea, and all of it consists of her words. I left in the few mistakes I saw.

She began writing this by hand, then she typed it into her iPhone using the 'Notes' app, after which she texted it to me.

All things considered, I think she did a marvelous job. She even wrote the 'about the author' section by herself.

Chapter One
THE YEAR OF 2020

The year of 2020 started off normal, until March. After spring break, we had no school because of coronavirus.

We had no school for a while, then we had to start home school. Around August, we started going back to school and had to wear masks in public.

School was very different because of coronavirus. We had some kids going to school, and some kids doing more home school. Here are a few things that are different about school: we had to wear masks, we could not mix classes, and we were only allowed to sit two people per seat on the bus.

When coronavirus was announced, the grocery stores were almost out of stock.

Some of the main items that were almost out of stock were toilet paper, paper towels, cleaning supplies, hand sanitizer, and masks.

People were in the grocery stores buying stuff that would last them a few weeks or more. This kept going on through March and May.

Then, most places closed because of coronavirus. Most of the restaurants and stores closed. We had to use services like DoorDash if we wanted to eat from restaurants. Eventually, some places opened back up but would not let us inside.

This year, we also had to elect a new president, and millions of people had to mail their votes instead of voting in person. If you went in person to vote, you had to wear a mask, and you had to make sure you stayed away from the other people.

Chapter Two
COVID CHANGES

There are some changes we had to go through because of COVID, and here are six of them:

- COVID made us quarantine.
- COVID made us wear masks.
- COVID made us stay six feet apart.
- COVID made it so we couldn't have parties.
- COVID made it so we couldn't do sports.
- And worst of all, COVID made it so we couldn't play with friends.

These are only a few changes. There are a lot more changes COVID made us go through.

This is also some of many reasons why 2020 was the worst year ever.

Chapter Three
HOW IT'S GETTING BETTER

COVID might have put us through many changes, but things are getting better. Here are six things that are getting better:

- Places are opening back up, allowing us to go to stores and other areas.
- Grocery stores are stocked up again, so we don't have to worry about getting food.
- We are allowed to play with friends again.
- We have vaccines, which will make us better.
- We have vaccine pods.
- And we are allowed to have parties.

There are only a couple more things getting better about COVID because the pandemic is still going on.

Chapter Four
EXTRA

This book was written during the pandemic of COVID-19. COVID was not just in the year 2020. It started in the end of 2019 and has continued on to 2021. Some people say it might continue on to 2022. COVID is a really bad pandemic because of how many people it has killed.

Scientists and doctors have made three different vaccines. Hopefully, the vaccines will help stop COVID.

Chapter Five
2020 THE WORST

Last year—2020—was the worst year I have lived through so far. COVID ruined the year because of all the changes it caused. It made 2020 the worst! I really did not like 2020. I wish it never happened.

ABOUT THE AUTHOR

I am eight years old and in third grade, and I used my experiences to write this book. I plan on writing more books with what I know and my experiences. I enjoy writing fiction books, so I will probably write some fiction books and nonfiction books. My grandpa is a writer and I hope me and him both become famous writers. I hope my dream comes true.

www.ingramcontent.com/pod-product-compliance
Lightning Source LLC
Chambersburg PA
CBHW042113120526
44592CB00042B/2796